C0-BEH-864

American Association of Collegiate Registrars and Admissions Officers

SEM
CORE
CONCEPTS

Building Blocks for Institutional and Student Success

By Wayne Sigler, Ed.D.

American Association of Collegiate
Registrars and Admissions Officers
One Dupont Circle, NW, Suite 520
Washington, DC 20036-1135

Tel: (202) 293-9161 | Fax: (202) 872-8857 | www.aacrao.org

For a complete listing of AACRAO publications, visit www.aacrao.org/
publications.

The American Association of Collegiate Registrars and Admissions Officers,
founded in 1910, is a nonprofit, voluntary, professional association of more
than 11,000 higher education administrators who represent more than 2,600
institutions and agencies in the United States and in forty countries around
the world. The mission of the Association is to provide leadership in policy
initiation, interpretation, and implementation in the global educational
community. This is accomplished through the identification and promotion of
standards and best practices in enrollment management, information technology, instructional management, and student services.

©Copyright 2017 American Association of Collegiate Registrars and
Admissions Officers. All rights reserved. No part of this publication may be
reproduced in any form without permission in writing from AACRAO.

AACRAO adheres to the principles of non-discrimination without regard to
age, color, handicap or disability, ethnic or national origin, race, religion, gender
(including discrimination taking the form of sexual harassment), marital,
parental or veteran status, or sexual orientation.

**LIBRARY OF CONGRESS
CATALOGING-IN-PUBLICATION DATA**

Names: American Association of Collegiate Registrars and Admissions
Officers, issuing body.

Title: SEM core concepts : building blocks for institutional and student
success.

Description: Washington, DC : American Association of Collegiate Registrars
and Admissions Officers, [2017] | Includes bibliographical references and
index.

Identifiers: LCCN 2017005081 | ISBN 9781578581184 (pbk.)

Subjects: LCSH: Universities and colleges--United States--Admission.
College attendance--United States--Planning.
School enrollment--United States.

Classification: LCC LB2351.2 .S45 2017 | DDC 378.1/01--dc23

LC record available at https://lccn.loc.gov/2017005081

Table of Contents

i

Acknowledgments

SEM Core Concepts reflects the thinking and practices of many of the people who have, over the years, made strategic enrollment management (SEM) a major contributor to the ability of colleges and universities to successfully carry out their missions. This publication is written with the goal of letting these experts speak in their own unique voices.

Special acknowledgment goes to the late Bob Bontrager, former senior director of AACRAO Consulting and SEM Initiatives. Before assuming that position, he was the assistant provost for enrollment management at Oregon State University. Bob was a SEM practitioner and thought leader who made significant contributions to the development of SEM as a profession, some of which are included in this publication. He left us far too early, at age 58, after a valiant battle with cancer.

A hearty thank you goes to the all-star cast of SEM thought leaders, practitioners, and academics that generously gave their time and expertise to the production of this publication:

- Jay Goff, Vice President of Enrollment and Retention Management, St. Louis University
- Susan Gottheil, Vice Provost (Students), University of Manitoba (Canada)
- Don Hossler, Distinguished Provost Professor Emeritus, School of Education, Indiana University
- David Kalsbeek, Senior Vice President, Division of Enrollment Management and Marketing, DePaul University
- Donald Norris, Founder and President, Strategic Initiatives, Inc., Reston, Virginia
- Michele Sandlin, Managing Consultant, AACRAO Consulting

Special thanks also goes to the following colleagues for their significant assistance in the development of this publication through their expert advice and several rounds of editing:

- Tom Green, Associate Executive Director, AACRAO Consulting and SEM. Tom was a strong proponent of this project, provided very helpful advice throughout the project, and was a key resource for various portions of the document.

- Stanley Henderson, Vice Chancellor for Enrollment Management and Student Life, University of Michigan, Dearborn (retired). Stan has been a practitioner, thought leader, and major nurturer of SEM since its very early stages. He is the author of Chapter Two, "The Evolution of SEM."

- Christine Kerlin, Vice President of Enrollment Management and Director of the University Center, Everett Community College (Washington) (retired). Christine is a highly respected SEM practitioner and thought leader with an emphasis on community colleges.

- Clayton Smith, Associate Professor, Faculty of Education, University of Windsor (Canada). Clayton is an experienced and respected SEM practitioner in both Canadian and U.S. colleges and universities and co-author of *SEM in Canada*. He is also Director of AACRAO's Strategic Enrollment Management Conference.

Special appreciation goes to the following colleagues for the privilege of co-leading with them the "Core Concepts of SEM" workshops at several AACRAO national SEM conferences. These individuals significantly contributed to my thinking about the various aspects of SEM.

- Brent Gage, Associate Vice President for Enrollment Management, University of Iowa
- Jody Gordon, Vice President, Students and Enrollment Management, University of the Fraser Valley (Canada)
- Alicia Moore, Dean of Student and Enrollment Services, Central Oregon Community College

Finally, special recognition also goes to Michael Reilly, AACRAO Executive Director, for his support of this project, Martha Henebry, AACRAO Director of Operations, Membership and Publications, for initiating this project and for her expert, tireless, and patient shepherding of it from start to finish, and to Jessica Montgomery for her terrific expertise in editing and coaching the author to fine tune this publication.

Wayne Sigler, Ed.D.

About the Author

Dr. Wayne Sigler is a nationally-respected enrollment management practitioner, consultant, author and speaker. He served as vice president for enrollment management and chief enrollment officer at George Mason University from July 2012 until July 2014, where he was asked to lead the development and implementation of a new university-wide comprehensive and coordinated strategic enrollment management program.

Prior to joining Mason, Dr. Sigler served as director of admissions at the University of Minnesota-Twin Cities for 20 years, building an undergraduate admissions program that is regarded as one of the elite programs in both the Big Ten and the United States. Under his leadership, the University realized a 63-percent increase in new freshman enrollment, including strong increases in the academic preparation and diversity of the freshman class.

Before joining the University of Minnesota, Dr. Sigler served as dean of admissions and assistant vice president for enrollment services at the University of Houston, dean of student and academic services at Southwest Texas State University (now Texas State University, San Marcos), director of undergraduate admissions at the University of Maryland, College Park and associate director of admissions at Towson State College (now Towson University).

Dr. Sigler has had a significant influence on the national enrollment management movement. He developed the nationally recognized Tri-O leadership/management system that is stakeholder-focused and outcomes-oriented. He is the author of the book, *Managing for Change: Shifting from Process-Centric to Results-Oriented Operations* (AACRAO 2007), and he chaired AACRAO's Enrollment Management Committee several times and participated in the development of AACRAO's Strategic Enrollment Management (SEM) Conference. In 2008, Dr. Sigler received the AACRAO APEX Award that recognizes excellence in education administration and outstanding achievement and influence in the profession. He also served a two-year term as president of the Association of Chief Admissions Officers of Public Universities (ACAOPU), a professional organization for the chief admissions officers of the nation's flagship public universities.

Sigler earned a B.S. in Political Science from Towson State College and both an M.A. in Education and a Ed.D. in Higher Education from The George Washington University.

Introduction

Strategic enrollment management (SEM) has evolved over the 40 years since its inception to become a powerful system for enabling colleges and universities to take better control of their enrollment destiny. The myriad of challenges that higher education currently faces make it imperative that the leadership at all levels of an institution fully understand how SEM can help to proactively address these challenges. Reduced funding in many states, declining numbers of high school graduates, expectations from students and their families for demonstrated outcomes and return on their investment, and the importance of serving an increasing diversification of students present a challenge for higher education leaders.

SEM Core Concepts is designed to provide busy professionals with a macro overview of SEM. Whether or not an institution is already using SEM practices, this guide will be a helpful resource for establishing or building on an existing SEM program.

The guide is organized around the following topics:

- Definitions of SEM and examples of what it is not
- The evolution of SEM, including its developmental stages that provided the building blocks for the current best practices of the profession
- An overview of the essential SEM concepts
- A planning model and road map for transforming an institution into a SEM organization

This publication is not intended to be a how-to guide or a definitive exploration of SEM. While there is not a definitive definition of SEM best practices, based on my 40 years in the enrollment profession as a practitioner, consultant, and author, I have designated as "core concepts" those ideas that seem to be lasting and often-referenced, and as "best practice" those practices that currently seem to be viewed with general agreement in the profession. Additional resources are listed at the end of the publication.

Chapter One:

What is SEM?

A number of definitions of strategic enrollment management (SEM) have been developed by academics and practitioners since its inception.[1][2] Three of the most widely accepted include:

1. "A **concept** and **process** that enables the fulfillment of institutional mission and students' educational goals" (Bontrager 2009, 18).

---

[1] The terms enrollment management (EM) and strategic enrollment management (SEM) are used interchangeably in this publication. The early adopters and observers of the concept generally referred to it as enrollment management. As the profession developed, the term strategic enrollment management became more prevalent to reflect both the holistic and institution-wide nature of the concept and to identify SEM as primarily strategic rather than tactical.

[2] Increasingly, colleges and universities are addressing the enrollment future of their institution by establishing EM offices and/or EM units or divisions within their institutions. The responsibilities assigned to these structures vary widely, reflecting both an institution's perception of its challenges and opportunities and its culture and resources. Since the titles of the persons heading the SEM programs vary from institution to institution, this publication generally uses the term "SEM leader" except for quotations from sources.

> "A **concept** and **process** that enables the fulfillment of institutional mission and students' educational goals"
>
> *(Bontrager 2009, 18)*

2. "A **comprehensive** and **coordinated process** that enables a college to identify enrollment goals that are aligned with its multiple missions, its strategic plan, its enrollment, and its resources, and to reach those goals through the effective integration of administrative processes, student services, curriculum planning, and market analysis" (Kerlin 2008, 11).

3. "Both an **organizational concept** as well as a **systematic set of activities** designed to enable educational institutions to exert more influence over their student enrollments and total net tuition revenue derived from enrolled students. Organized by strategic planning and supported by institutional research, enrollment management activities concern student college choice, transition to college, student attrition and retention, and student outcomes. These

processes are studied to guide institutional practices in the areas of new student recruitment and financial aid, student support services, curriculum development and other academic areas that affect enrollments, student persistence, and student outcomes from college" (Hossler 2011, 70).

What SEM Is Not

To fully understand SEM, it is important to know what it is not. It is not:[3]

1. **A quick fix.** SEM primarily focuses on strategic rather than tactical issues and concentrates on systemic and foundational solutions. It generally takes six to nine months to develop a comprehensive and effective SEM plan and approximately three years to get a new SEM program fully operational. If executed properly, incremental improvements in outcomes should occur during the implementation stages.

   SEM exists in a fast-paced, high-stakes climate of ongoing demands for results. Therefore, while developing and implementing a SEM plan, it is vital that SEM professionals remember that their top priority is meeting enrollment targets for the upcoming terms. Successful SEM practitioners are pragmatic and learn to be com-

---

[3] The list of "What SEM Is Not" has evolved over the years. An early version (and possibly the original list) was developed by Bontrager (2004). It was modified by others, often AACRAO practitioners presenting workshops and sessions on SEM. The author chose to use the list from Green, T. 2016 (April). Strategic Enrollment Management Quarterly, edited by T. C. Green and H. Zimar. Retrieved from: <http://onlinelibrary.wiley.com/journal/10.1002/(ISSN)2325-4750>.

fortable working on immediate priorities and, at the same time, on longer-term plans that are a work in progress.

2. **An enhanced admission and marketing operation.** Recruitment, admission, and marketing often come to mind when discussing SEM. While those are important components of SEM, an effective SEM program also actively focuses on promoting student academic success, engagement, and development through the entire student enrollment life cycle—from prospective student through engaged alumnus.

3. **An administrative function separate from the academic mission of the institution.** Michael Dolence points out that "an institution's academic program is inexorably co-dependent on enrollment management. The quality of the academic program can only be developed and maintained in a stable environment, and stable enrollments are only possible through sound planning" (1993, 9). SEM is embedded in the academic fabric of an institution to support the work of faculty and students through services such as promoting academic programs, ensuring smooth and accurate registration and records, coordinating academic advising, tutoring, career planning, and designing and managing the classroom set up to facilitate learning. Through the academic leadership of the insti-

> The focus of best practice SEM is not on a hierarchal structure and control but on facilitating consultation and the successful development, coordination, and implementation of strategies.

tution, best practice SEM programs actively engage the faculty in discussions about curriculum and program planning, and the impacts of various teaching and learning approaches on the academic success of students. This often includes assessing course design and delivery modes and employing evolving relevant research findings and technology to support teaching, advising, and mentoring approaches.

4. **Solely an organizational structure.** While important to SEM success, organizational structure is a means to an end that supports the achievement of an institution's mission and student success. The focus of best practice SEM is not on a hierarchal structure and control but on facilitating consultation and the successful development, coordination, and implementation of strategies.

5. **A financial drain on the institutional budget.** While implementing an ef-

fective SEM program can be a significant investment of institutional time and money, best practice SEM leaders employ technology, process reengineering, service surveys and metrics, and ROI studies to help ensure both efficiency and effectiveness. SEM has a stronger chance of being successful if the focus is kept on achieving the expected return on investment (ROI).

Chapter Two:

The Evolution of SEM[4]

The history of SEM is one of evolution. SEM professionals have taken admissions from a focus on gatekeeping a high number of applicants, to shaping the profile of the entering freshmen class, to ensuring that institutions represent and provide opportunity for a broad cross-section of the geographic areas from which they draw. They have also turned the traditional admission funnel on its side and created a "cradle-to-endowment" approach to the student enrollment life cycle; created seamless services; and applied strategy, data, and technology to student success.

Early SEM efforts focused on the intake of students through recruitment and marketing. As SEM has evolved, it has increasingly

[4] Special recognition goes to Stanley E. Henderson, Vice Chancellor for Enrollment Management & Student Life, University of Michigan, Dearborn (retired), for writing this chapter (with the exception of "SEM Challenges," which was written by the author). Stan is uniquely qualified for this task because of his involvement with SEM since its beginning and his major influence on its development as a practitioner, author, AACRAO's first Vice President for Enrollment Management, and former AACRAO President. Thank you, Stan!

moved further through the student enrollment life cycle into student progression, retention, persistence, completion, and outcomes. In the process, it has become more than the sum of its parts and the result has been transformational.

1970s: In the Beginning— "Grand Designs" and Marketing Roots

In 1974, with the Baby Boom gone bust, Boston College's Frank Campanella challenged his young admissions dean, Jack Maguire, to implement a vision of integrated functions that could turn the enrollment tide. He assured Maguire that what he called "enrollment management" (EM) would "require a coordinated and integrated effort of the highest order" (Campanella 1974). Maguire's resultant "grand design" incorporated outstanding people using the right information in the right organizational structure to create a synergy that still defines the EM concept today. A primary focus of early EM was marketing, seen in the late '70s as a "comprehensive rather than singular approach to conception and implementation" that could shape new organizational structures to meet student needs (Huddleston 1980). What was needed was an administrative component that could more effectively articulate and communicate what an institution could do for prospective and current students. The result was an innovative structure that went beyond admissions and financial aid into other student services that would eventually define the "cradle-to-endowment" approach to EM.

1980s: Building EM Structure

By 1982, Kemerer, Baldridge, and Green were identifying a continuum of structures, each expressing a progressively more complex system of EM, to deliver the promise of EM. These "structural strategists" created the quintessential EM forms that became benchmarks for identifying the level of EM development on a campus. These are further discussed in Chapter Four.

In the mid-1980s, Don Hossler was introducing his research on student college choice to EM in order to show how research could inform practice, as well as affirming that practice can shape research. EM "is not simply an administrative process. [It] involves the entire campus" (Hossler 1986, 70). He argued for a "new level of professionalism vis-à-vis a sound knowledge base and the need for a strong research and planning effort" (Hossler 1986, 70) that would require new skill sets and training for enrollment professionals.

1990s: Putting "Strategic" into EM

By 1990 Hossler and Bean were describing EM as "an organizational concept and a systematic set of activities designed to enable education institutions to exert more influence over their student enrollments" (1990, 5). At the same time, Michael Dolence was incorporating his institutional strategic planning background into EM. His contributions would focus EM into "a comprehensive process designed to help an institution achieve and maintain the optimum recruitment, retention, and graduation rates of students, where 'optimum' is defined within the academic context of the institution. As such, SEM is an institution-wide process that embraces virtually every aspect of an institution's function and culture" (Dolence 1993, 8). This focus on academics was the core of SEM (Dolence 1993). Dolence's view is not just student-centered, but *learner*-centered (Gottheil and Smith 2011; Henderson 2001).

In creating the first AACRAO SEM primer, Dolence (1993) provided a template of goals and critical success factors for measuring success in SEM that institutions could use to evaluate their EM efforts. This also helped to propel AACRAO into the professional development of SEM.

2000s: Embedding SEM in Higher Education

Twenty-six years since its first meeting, the AACRAO SEM conference continues to provide cutting-edge theory, practice, and research for enrollment professionals and administrators. SEM also spawned AACRAO Consulting, a service for SEM planning and practice.

The SEM concept has now been widely adopted within higher education by community colleges, baccalaureate institutions, graduate schools, and professional programs. While using SEM core concepts as their guide, these groups have implemented their own take on SEM to fit their missions.

Gottheil and Smith, influential SEM leaders in Canada, observed that "shaping enrolment through a focused approach to student recruitment and retention is now acknowledged by many Canadian educators as an essential part of the higher education landscape" (2011, 3). They note that while the emergence of SEM in Canada has been more recent, "the experience of Canadian enrolment professionals demonstrates that many of the issues facing Canadian colleges and universities are similar to those of American institutions. Yet Canadian history and value systems have also shaped a distinctive approach to SEM that has resulted in different areas of focus and different strategies and tactics to influence student recruitment and retention" (Gottheil and Smith 2011, 3). This led to the creation of Canada's own SEM meeting, the Canadian SEM Summit, which will celebrate its 10th offering in 2017.

This professionalization of SEM also positioned the concept to move into the international higher education scene. Countries around the world are increasingly dealing with the challenges of managing enrollments and higher education funding—in many places moving from free to tuition-driven institutions. While recruitment tools and financial aid practices may be very different, educators abroad have come to recognize the value of SEM's strategic approach to managing enrollments in the academic context.

> *The expansion of SEM outside North America has largely seen its practice evolve along lines similar to the origins of SEM. Many institutions grappling with shifting demographics and issues of access to higher education for groups historically less likely to enroll and pressured by shrinking resources and rising costs have turned to SEM concepts as a means to exert greater control over their enroll-*

ment destinies. Most of this work begins with the analysis of student needs and markets, followed by systematic recruitment and marketing, often new concepts for these institutions. Many of these university systems are highly decentralized, making systematic approaches more challenging and less likely to leverage the combined resources of the entire institution. (Green 2016b)

SEM has always been rooted in the analysis and use of data to inform and improve decision making. However, in the early 2000s, SEM was drawing on technology and analytics in enrollment practices, which drew criticism from many that SEM was putting the emphasis on rankings and metrics that did not position higher education to play the role of widening opportunity (Haycock 2006). In response, Bontrager (2006) sought to demonstrate that SEM could help institutions achieve clarity on priorities arising from their mission, as well as meet societal goals of access for underrepresented students.

By 2005, Henderson was arguing that SEM had become "stuck on structure" and needed to refocus on the academic context (2005, 4). The institution that looked at enrollments through the academic lens of its culture and mission could avoid the practice of SEM for the sake of meeting enrollment goals without regard for student success. Combining academic mission with SEM practice could position a campus to meet student access and

focus on student success—while also achieving enrollment success (Henderson 2005).

Today: Integrating SEM's Roots

As SEM approaches its fifth decade, there has been an increasing emphasis on the integration of its roots. Kalsbeek (2006) suggests that four broad orientations to SEM — student-focused, administrative, academic, and market-centered — can help to ensure that the expectations of the different stakeholders are addressed. Each of these orientations frames how SEM is conceived, defined, organized, implemented, and evaluated.[5] Smith and Kilgore (2006) and Henderson and Yale (2008) speak to the importance of recognizing the "faces" of SEM that must be integrated for a successful SEM: administrative-structural; planning; and leadership. Henderson (2012) adds a "community face" that brings relationships to bear as the driving force for making sure that the different voices within the colleges and universities are taken into consideration. These are SEM's data, analytical, research, and structural toolsets.

Today's higher education environment puts SEM squarely in the vortex created by governmental and public accountability and the competition for scarce students. How well enrollment managers can integrate the roots of SEM that have evolved in the last 40 years will be the true test of their continuing ability to transform their campuses as the future unfolds.

[5] David Kalsbeek addressed the "Four Orientations of SEM" in three related articles (parts one, two, and three) in *College and University*. They are cited in the Bibliography.

SEM Challenges

The significant changes taking place in higher education constitute what is often called the "new normal." It is characterized by the now familiar theme that higher education will never go back to many of the conditions and practices that were previously in place. Institutions of higher education will need to continually evolve in market-valued and academically-sound ways to stay financially viable and equipped to meet the needs of their students. Institutional SEM leaders are expected to assume a major role in successfully addressing these challenges.

Some of today's most compelling SEM-related challenges include:

1. Improving student access, engagement, retention, development, and graduation.

2. Responding to changing demographic populations, including increasing numbers of persons of color, indigenous, first-generation, and economically-disadvantaged students.

3. Recognizing that postsecondary education can no longer associate student lack of achievement with lack of will. This calls for providing a more welcoming and inclusive campus culture and more tailored and effective academic and student support services.

4. Declining number of high school graduates in many states and uneven population growth across geographic areas.

5. Increased competition among institutions, including in student recruitment, rankings, and ratings.

6. Decreased funding from most states and at the federal level.

7. Reduction in demand for some academic programs and increased demand that exceeds capacity in some other majors.

8. Demand for accountability and demonstrated institutional effectiveness and return on investment from higher education by students, parents, donors, foundations, accrediting agencies, and federal and state governments.

9. Increasing demand for more comprehensive career services.

10. Market vulnerability associated with continued significant increases in tuition and fees. (Gage and Sigler 2016)

Chapter Three:

Implementing SEM

SEM is often described as a concept or a construct. The following are tangible examples of how the purposes of SEM are achieved. The examples listed below can also be considered best practices and benchmarks for establishing effective SEM practices.[6]

Establishing Clear Goals

Three primary enrollment-related goals are found in most institutional enrollment plans: the number of new students, diversity (broadly defined), and the academic profile (academic preparation). Typically, these goals are set at the trustee, senior institutional leadership,

---

[6] This list was developed for a workshop titled "Building the Foundation for SEM Success" at the 2016 AACRAO Strategic Enrollment Management conference (Gage and Sigler 2016). The list has been slightly modified for this publication and some of the narrative on this topic draws on Bob Bontrager (2004), except as otherwise noted. Bontrager's list titled "The Core Concepts of Enrollment Management" is possibly the original version of this subject. It has likely been refined, over time, by various professionals for presentations on this topic. The last two items in the list were developed by the author.

> It is in the process of helping senior campus administrators and boards of trustees to understand, define, prioritize, and balance these institutional goals that we locate the heart and soul of any enrollment management strategy.

and/or school/college/faculty levels. All but the most selective institutions (those with a significant surplus of qualified applicants to meet their enrollment targets) face difficulty in attempting to meet all three targets on a regular basis.

Increasingly, goals for retention are also being set as institutions seek to improve students' academic performance and graduation rates. For public institutions, especially those with very competitive admissions standards, the percentage of in-state versus nonresident student enrollment targets often competes with political and tuition revenue priorities. SEM theorists Hossler and Kalsbeek (2008, 6) add that:

> *The enrollment goals of senior campus administrators are almost always multifaceted and complex; they also are almost always in conflict with one another…. the six primary and overarching goals found at most campuses [are]: improving market position and market demand, enhancing the academic profile of the student body, ensuring the economic diversity of the student body, ensuring racial/ethnic diversity, improving persistence and graduation rates, and increasing net tuition revenue… But at the crux of the strategic nature of enrollment management goals is the fact that the simultaneous pursuit of all these goals requires a difficult balancing act not only of resources but of competing outcomes; [and] it requires the management of multiple trade-offs since in many ways these enrollment goals are in conflict and often mutually incompatible. We suggest that it is in the process of helping senior campus administrators and boards of trustees to understand, define, prioritize, and balance these institutional goals that we locate the heart and soul of any enrollment management strategy.*

The process of setting reasonable, consistent, and clear enrollment-related goals will likely always be challenging, but the process can be made smoother and more realistic by some of the approaches addressed in this publication. The development of a best practice data-supported SEM plan, discussed in Chapter Five, can be especially helpful in this process.

Improving Student Access, Transition, Persistence, and Graduation

The core mission of any college and university is academic and student success. Best practice SEM leaders understand that recruitment,

Figure 1. The "Classic" Admissions Funnel

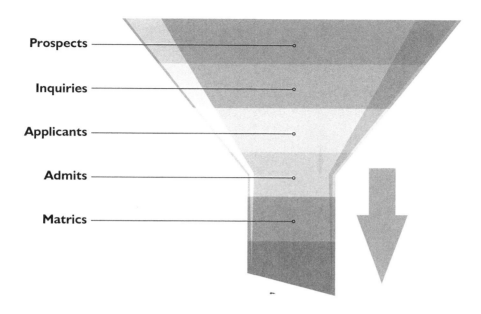

Prospects

Inquiries

Applicants

Admits

Matrics

Source: University of Iowa Division of Enrollment Management

retention, and graduation are equally important in achieving institutional mission and,
ideally, equal attention should be devoted to
the three objectives. The approach to achieving
these objectives has evolved over the years. The
following are models that trace the evolution
of the SEM approach to improving students
access, transition, persistence, and graduation.

Figure 1 displays the "classic" admissions
funnel that served for decades as the primary
model for recruiting a new class and viewing
enrollment projections. Student access and a
positive transition to the institution were important goals of the emerging EM profession
and continue to be a priority. The admissions
funnel model is still relevant and in use by
most institutions for this purpose. However,
the model is now viewed as too narrow in fo-

The core mission of any
college and university is academic and student success.
Best practice SEM leaders
understand that recruitment,
retention, and graduation are
equally important in achieving
institutional mission and, ideally, equal attention should be
devoted to the three objectives.

Figure 2. Traditional Enrollment Perspective

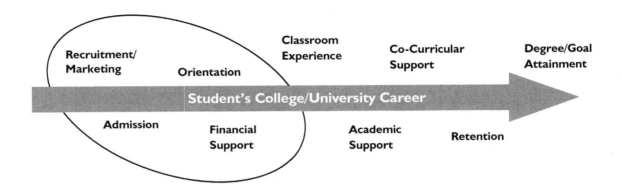

Source: Bontrager (2011).

cus because it does not reflect the much more comprehensive nature of SEM.

Figure 2, the "traditional enrollment perspective," portrays a more complete understanding of the full student enrollment life cycle continuum that came into play as the EM profession developed. The limitations of this model are (1) the focus is still on the early stages of enrollment as indicated by the circle in this model and (2) the student services provided by colleges and universities throughout the student enrollment life cycle are often somewhat siloed rather than seamless.

"The SEM perspective," depicted in Figure 3, calls for institutions to more fully address the complete life cycle of the student experience rather than primarily focusing on the recruiting, admission, and onboarding phases. Current best practice SEM envisions that institutions give equal attention

to recruitment, student success (expanded to include retention, student development, and a positive student experience), and graduation. This model also envisions that each of the institutional units that work with students at various phases of the enrollment life cycle will transition from a siloed approach to a more coordinated, collaborative, and synergistic effort to help students move successfully and seamlessly through each stage.

Tom Green (2016b) points out that the SEM perspective model reflects an understanding that:

> With this perspective, institutional leaders assess the experiences of their students, typically finding that different types of students experience the institution differently than others. For example, the needs of special populations of students, those at greatest risk to leave before reaching their

Figure 3. The SEM Perspective

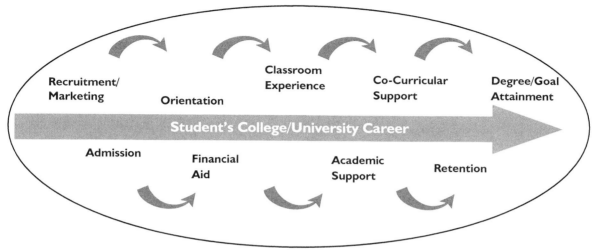

Source: Bontrager (2011).

educational goals, are an important part of overall institutional success. These may include students whose academic preparation was insufficient to ensure initial success, those whose culture and heritage make it harder for them to integrate into the fabric of the institution, those who lack financial resources or strong family support, adults who balance work/career/family/community with institutional demands, etc. By identifying those groups and creating effective support systems and services, their success rates can improve and, very often, lift overall institutional success rates.

Strategic and Financial Planning

SEM is primarily strategic rather than tactical. Marketing and strategy expert Eugene Michaelson describes strategy as "thought seeking its means of execution," while tactics are "the means to carry out the desires of thought" (1987, 3). He emphasizes that the strategy must be correct for the organization to succeed.

> The strategy must be right first; then the tactics can support the strategy. Excellent strategy at higher levels can sustain many tactical failures at lower levels. The converse is rarely true. Sustained tactical success—even continuous brilliant execution of tactics—seldom overcomes an inadequate strategic posture. A bad strategy supported by good tactics can even be a fast route to failure as, for example, driving fast and skillfully in the wrong direction does not get you to your destination. (Michaelson 1987, 5)

At its best, SEM is data-informed. To make their work effective and efficient and to reduce risk, best practice SEM professionals increasingly employ data, metrics, and analytics to combine a quantitative, data- and research-driven approach (the "science") with a qualitative approach to making decisions based on experience, context, knowledge, and judgment developed through working in the profession (the "art"). Strategically harnessing the power of metrics and analytics in SEM programs can provide institutions with a major competitive advantage.

Chapter Five includes key information on the role of various enrollment-related strategic and tactical plans.

The purpose of SEM is sometimes thought of as primarily bringing in funds for the institution by student enrollments. While this viewpoint vastly overlooks the comprehensive mission of SEM, there is no question that funds really matter. It is impossible to accomplish the institution's mission and support student success without adequate funding. A shortfall of tuition and other funds can quickly place an institution in a crisis situation.

It is imperative that the senior institutional leaders, including the provost, chief financial officer, chief enrollment management officer, and the chief student affairs officer work closely in order to conduct proactive and successful strategic and financial planning. The following factors are essential to achieve this:

A. **Transparency of budgets and unit operations.** In order to make informed recommendations and decisions, all senior institutional leaders should have a clear understanding of the mission, challenges, effectiveness, and the operating budgets of the other units.

B. **An understanding that each division has a significant stake in the success of the other units, namely:**

    I. The process of developing institutional and divisional budgets, as well as financial aid and scholarship budgets is high stakes, complex, and politically sensitive, and should be informed by research and analytical modeling. Each senior institutional officer should fully understand how these decisions are reached and the implications for each division.

    II. It is now becoming relatively commonplace for the chief financial officer and the chief SEM leader to work closely to prepare for and present at meetings with the external institutional credit rating funds.

Figure 4. Application to Strategic Enrollment Management (SEM)

	Type of Analytics or Reporting	Focus	Application to Strategy
Analytics	Optimization	What's the best that can happen?	Refine SEM strategies, targets, practices, and actions to achieve optimal outcomes.
	Predictive Modeling	What will happen next?	Sophisticated predictive modeling shapes recruitment, yield, and retention policies and practices.
	Forecasting/ Extrapolation	What if these trends continue?	Forecasting SEM strategies and outcomes.
	Statistical Analysis	Why is this happening?	Current and longitudinal analysis to support refinement and execution of SEM strategy.
Query & Reporting	Alerts	What actions are needed?	Alerts and interventions, based on both predictive modeling and actual current performance and level of engagement.
	Query/Drill Down	Where exactly is the problem?	Capacity to drill down to examine individual learners based on dynamic viewing of cohorts.
	Ad Hoc Reports	How many, how often, where?	Capacity to expand list of variables and dynamically view cohorts and individual learners using many variables.
	Standard Reports	What happened?	Standard portfolio of reports and views most needed by decision makers.

Source: Norris (n.d., 21).

Creating a Data-Rich Environment

At its best, SEM is data-informed. To make their work effective and efficient and to reduce risk, best practice SEM professionals increasingly employ data, metrics, and analytics to combine a quantitative, data- and research-driven approach (the "science") with a qualitative approach to making decisions based on experience, context, knowledge, and judgment developed through working in the profession (the "art"). Strategically harnessing the power of metrics and analytics in SEM programs can provide institutions with a major competitive advantage.

Figure 4 provides an overview of the types of metrics and analytics that are essential components of a best practice SEM program. Metrics involve tools that measure and focus on results, while analytics provide an interpretation and communication of meaningful patterns in data.

Key Success Indicators

SEM practitioners rely heavily on metrics often called key enrollment indicators (KEIs) and key performance indicators (KPIs) to guide their work. KEIs define institutional goals such as enrollment, the percentage of new first-year students who enroll as sophomores, the percentage of students who graduate in four years, and net tuition revenue. KPIs define internal operational targets and standards such as turnaround time for decisions on financial aid applications or response times to incoming emails and calls. KEIs and KPIs can also serve as an early warning system to enable SEM professionals to assess whether a process or projects is on track to achieve a specified goal, target, or standard, and to take timely corrective action when it is needed.

Analytics

In recent years, the use of analytics in SEM has increased exponentially. The following are examples of the types of analytical modeling that are becoming best practices:

1. Guiding the strategic use of financial aid and scholarship funds to support the achievement of the institution's mission to help students with financial need to attend and to meet enrollment and fiscal targets;
2. Assessing the effectiveness of various recruitment activities and operational processes;
3. Predicting which prospects are most likely to enroll;
4. Determining which geographic markets hold the most potential for the institution's enrollment efforts; and
5. Supporting the development and operation of student success programs.

Improving Processes and Outcomes

The continual improvement of process, organizational and financial effectiveness, efficiency, and outcomes is a major component of a best practices SEM program. This improvement is necessary for SEM professionals to be good stewards of institutional resources and demonstrate a specific and measurable return on investment.

Process is one of the vital ways that the outcomes of SEM are achieved. It provides the structure, order, and predictability that are absolutely essential to any well-run organization (Sigler 2016). Some processes are as simple as adding a class to a student's schedule. Other processes, such as recruiting an incoming class, are extremely complex.

It is important to stress, however, that SEM is highly goal-oriented and processes and activities are a means to an end, not an outcome unto themselves. Highly-effective SEM practitioners are focused on consistently achieving the outcomes valued and expected by their stakeholders. Understanding who the various stakeholders are, what results they value and expect, and being able to demonstrate the consistent delivery of those outcomes, helps ensure the success of the organizational unit and its practitioners.

Strengthening Communications and Collaboration Across Campus

Best practice SEM is not about a few administrative units, such as admissions, marketing, and financial aid. It requires commitment and contributions from all of the component units of the institution. "Options for aligning an institution's SEM processes, its organizational structure for decision making and continuous improvement, and its development of strategic enrollment plans with cross-campus input, integration, and buy in" (Bontrager and Green 2012) are discussed in Chapter Six.

Applying SEM Research

The poignant advice offered by comedian Will Rogers can apply to the SEM profession: "Even if you are on the right track, if you just sit there, you will get run over." A wide range of knowledge and application is demanded of today's SEM leaders. In order to successfully meet these expectations, the SEM leader must be a dedicated student of the profession and draw on both theoretical and applied research to inform their work. They benefit from an interdisciplinary array of research from a variety of disciplines such as the social sciences, business, neuroscience, data, and computer science. SEM practitioners who are in the vanguard of the profession choose to think "out of the box" to learn and adapt their work from the strategies and practices of fields that initially appear to be quite different from SEM, such as business, medicine, law enforcement, political science, and many others.

Harnessing Technology

Leading a successful SEM organization involves managing many, often very complex, processes and services. To support their work and to facilitate excellent operational service to stakeholders, most SEM offices make extensive use of technology solutions. These include client relationship management systems, enterprise-level student information systems, document imaging, transfer credit evaluations, degree planning and audits, and classroom and space management, to name a few.

Harnessing the power of technology to support and serve is usually not a simple task and is often a "two-sided coin." On the positive side, technology offers the potential for significant time and cost savings and service improvements that far outweigh the potential challenges such as:

1. The institutional politics of selecting technology that will adequately meet the needs of various institutional units and their stakeholders;
2. The cost of purchasing and installing the new software and equipment;
3. Significant training time and expense;
4. Failing to clearly specify and understand the outcomes that will be delivered by the technology (sometimes called adopting technology in search of a need);
5. System failures that become political and public relations problems; and
6. Data security issues.

In order to maximize the successful application of technology and avoid serious problems with it, successful SEM leaders proactively partner with experts and stakeholders outside the SEM unit for their advice and assistance. Timely access to skilled technology staff is a must for success in today's SEM organizations, as well as effectively working with outside vendors to identify and install targeted technology solutions in order to leverage internal resources.

Chapter Four:

SEM and the Institutional Culture

Four Orientations of SEM

As noted in Chapter Two, David Kalsbeek, an influential SEM practitioner and thought leader, identified four broad orientations to SEM that frame how SEM is conceived, defined, organized, implemented, and evaluated. They are: student-focused, administrative, academic, and market-centered. Kalsbeek suggests that "because each orientation represents a different set of core assumptions and presumptions about the nature of SEM, the result of a review of an issue from the multiple perspectives is likely to be a more robust and complete understanding of that issue" (2006).

Intended Outcomes of a SEM Strategy

Table 1 identifies Kalsbeek's views of the intended outcomes of EM strategy valued by the stakeholders of each of the four orientations to SEM.

The insights provided by the "four orientations of SEM" approach provide outstanding guidance for SEM leaders, who must, by

Table 1. Intended Outcomes of an Enrollment Management Strategy

Orientation of SEM	Intended Outcomes
Student-focused	Student engagement (from initial contact through recruitment and admissions, orientation, career and academic planning, extracurricular involvement, and persistence to degree) and student satisfaction.
Administrative	The most internally-focused of the four SEM orientations, the administrative orientation is concerned primarily with the processes and functions managed by the institution to effect enrollment goals. The primary outcomes valued by this orientation are the *efficiencies* and *effectiveness* of the institution's enrollment-related processes; primary focus will be given to return on investment measures, performance ratios, Key Performance Indicators and process metrics.
Academic	The focus of an academic orientation is not solely on the enrichment of student learning; rather, it extends to include the enrichment of the academic environment and academic programs—in short, the entire academic experience—through enrollment strategies that shape the profile, the process, and the product of the academic programs of an institution or a system.
Market-centered	In this orientation, the overarching purposes of enrollment management strategy are realized in terms of institutional market position. The most externally focused of the four SEM orientations; the outcomes are similarly externally focused. Enrollment management goals and outcomes are linked primarily to *elevating* and *enhancing* the institution's market position and leveraging its brand.

Source: Kalsbeek (2006b).

the nature of their position, build productive working relationships and coalitions with various institutional stakeholders, both on and off campus. SEM leaders can enhance the likelihood of a productive working relationship with their key stakeholders by understanding and taking into account their individual perspectives and expectations for the outcomes produced by the SEM program. Successful SEM leaders learn to candidly and creditably manage the expectations of their stakeholders about the projected outcomes of various projects.

Table 2. Models of Enrollment Management

Model	Degree of Restructuring Necessary	Authority
Committee	Low	Influence
Coordinator	Some	Networks
Matrix	Moderate	Cooperation
Division	High	Direct

Source: Penn (1999)

Organizing for SEM

There is no single "best practice" to institutionally organize for SEM. Each institution must develop the SEM structure that best fits its circumstances. This decision is likely to be based on factors such as the degree of urgency of focusing on enrollment, institutional culture, current administrative organizational structure, resources, internal political factors, and what is feasible at the time. The institution's type — such as community college, baccalaureate, or graduate and/or professional — will also play an important role in the SEM organization that is adopted.

Don Hossler, arguably the leading academic authority on SEM, stressed that:

> *An enrollment management system is an administrative structure. Colleges and universities, however, have two organizational structures: the more hierarchical and relatively tightly coupled administrative structures and the flat, more autonomous and loosely coupled faculty structure.* (1986, 37)

A comprehensive enrollment management plan should address the administrative structure of the institution as well as the role of the faculty. It should adopt a view of the student experience that links new student matriculation, new student adaptation, student persistence, and student outcomes. The factors that influence enrollments, however, are far too complex to be controlled or managed by any 'cookbook' approach to institutional management. (1986, 40)

Models of Enrollment Management

When the SEM profession was in its very early stages of development, Kemerer, Baldridge, and Green (1982) identified four possible models for organizing and coordinating enrollment activities: Institutional Marketing Committee, Staff Coordinator, Matrix Model, and Enrollment Management Division. In Table 2, the organizational models are de-

> There is no single "best practice" to institutionally organize for SEM. Each institution must develop the SEM structure that best fits its circumstances.

scribed in terms of the amount of organizational restructuring they require and the degree of authority they bestow. Models with little restructuring required tend to bestow less authority, while those with significant restructuring allocate the most centralized authority. A positive result for stakeholders is that the degree of accountability for expected outcomes increases as the level of authority increases.

The information outlined in Table 2 will be helpful for higher education leaders who want to conduct a social capital cost/benefit analysis of each model with respect to its fit for their institution and its current enrollment situation. Bontrager (2004) also provided helpful commentary on the institutional political implications of implementing the various models and the likely impact on enrollment by each model:

> *The main point about enrollment management organizations is this: enrollment results will generally depend on the structure adopted and institutions should adjust their expectations accordingly. When* enrollment issues are less pressing, institutions may be well served by the committee or coordinator approach. Institutional politics also may dictate adoption of these less intrusive models, though in that case decisions makers need to be prepared for more modest results. A desire for greater influence over enrollment results requires implementation of more significant structural changes.
>
> ***There is growing acknowledgment that implementation of the more significant structural changes required of the matrix or divisional models will lead to stronger enrollment results.*** *Institutional commitment to the concept of enrollment management is far greater with these models. They also take advantage of the emergence of enrollment professionals: individuals who have direct experience with one or more core enrollment operations, who have studied the growing body of enrollment management literature, [who] have been involved with the SEM community, and thus are uniquely qualified to lead campus enrollment efforts.* (Bontrager 2004, 14)

Variations on the Four Enrollment Models

There are, in actual practice, so many variations of the four models described above that it is very difficult to identify a "typical" organizational structure. However, some of the relatively recent variations on the four models are listed below.

1. The bursar and financial aid offices are increasingly included in the same organizational unit because of the close working relationship between these offices and the recognition that they are both student services.

2. In many cases, the registrar reports to the provost or student affairs, either directly or through an intermediate supervisor. Some institutions include the registrar in the enrollment services organizations or EM organization to promote a synergistic and coordinated approach to student services.

3. Some functions in the student affairs portfolio are receiving additional resources to address significant emerging student issues such as mental health/stress. Because of the major interest of students and parents regarding preparation for careers and the return on their expenditures for tuition and fees, many institutions are expanding the services and staffing in their career services unit.

4. Enrollment analytics staff are increasingly being added to various institutional research, reporting, and effectiveness units. In some cases, analytics staff are being added to SEM organizations. The impetus for this is often the heavy workload of the institutional research, reporting, and effectiveness unit and to enable the enrollment analytics staff to develop a thorough understanding of the specialized work and context of EM by being embedded with the SEM staff. Many institutions are turning to outside vendors to provide data analytics services when they don't have the resources to build this capability internally or they want to supplement the expertise of their on-campus services.

Chapter Five:

Enrollment-Related Plans

This section outlines the role of the three enrollment-related institutional plans: (1) overall institutional strategic plan, (2) SEM plan, and (3) SEM tactical action plans. Each plan should be distinctive in its focus, but complementary to the other plans.

As with much of the practice of SEM, each institution must decide what works best for its circumstances as it develops the three plans. To assist with the decision process, Figures 5 through 7 offer a combined SEM theoretical and practitioner perspective on the role and composition of each plan.

Institutional Strategic Plan

Most colleges and universities are familiar with institutional strategic plans. Many new presidents and chancellors initiate some form of a new strategic planning process that takes into account their vision for the institution. Figure 5 outlines the functions of the institutional strategic plan.

Figure 5. Institutional Strategic Plan

Institutional Strategic Plan
Purpose: master plan for the future direction of the institution: *Mission, Vision, Values, Strategic Goals*
Combination of concrete, inspirational, and aspirational.
Usually addresses the expectations of the institution's major stakeholders.
Answers macro questions such as What? Where? and Why?
Ideally, should identify the institution's competitive advantages and specify the institution's value propositions. The institution's major marketing and branding messages are often derived from this plan.
Generally updated every five to seven years, often initiated by new institutional leadership.

Strategic Enrollment Management Plan

The strategic enrollment management (SEM) plan is the strategic link that aligns tactical day-to-day enrollment and student success operations with the major strategic mission and goals outlined in the institutional strategic plan. Figure 6 lists the role of the SEM plan and its components.

Benefits of a SEM Plan
A comprehensive SEM plan requires six to nine months to be developed. Developing an effective SEM plan is well worth the effort for a number of reasons:

1. The process of writing a plan helps provide the necessary discipline of translating ideas into concrete actions.

> An effective SEM plan aids in goal setting because the research and analysis included in the plan help bring an informed perspective to the process of setting realistic versus aspirational goals.

2. It provides a vital learning process about the enrollment-related strengths and weaknesses of the institution and a useful perspective on the competition.

3. The process provides an excellent opportunity to draw on the talents and thinking of key segments of the

Figure 6. Strategic Enrollment Management Plan

Strategic Enrollment Management Plan

Purpose: focuses on comprehensive operational strategies to help achieve the mission and goals of the institution.

Usually more concrete and specific than the institutional strategic plan.

Answers, with more detail, questions such as What? Why? Where? and When?

1. Discusses enrollment goals, objectives, assessment criteria, and fiscal and physical capacity for institution and colleges/schools.
2. Strategically addresses each stage of the student enrollment life cycle from prospect through the alumni stage.
3. Should provide equal attention to student success and development, retention, and graduation as it does to recruitment.

Includes an environmental scan and institutional SWOT analysis to identify and evaluate:
- *Internal strengths and weaknesses*
- *External threats and opportunities*
- *The institution's competitive advantages and value propositions*
- *Market trends and competitive analysis*
- *Institution's position in the market*

This analysis is crucial to help shape realistic versus aspirational goals. It expands the focus of the institution beyond primarily recruitment and marketing to a much broader focus on the other key factors that drive enrollment.

Data-informed (information, metrics, analytics).

Draws on best practices.

Usually a three-to-five year plan to facilitate budget and facilities planning.
This is a living and learning document that continues to evolve and should be reviewed and updated yearly.

university and to develop and enhance productive working relationships with the stakeholders who will implement various aspects of the SEM process.

4. An effective SEM plan aids in goal setting because the research and analysis included in the plan help bring an informed perspective to the process of setting realistic versus aspirational goals.

Figure 7. SEM Tactical Action Plans

SEM Tactical Action Plans

Purpose: focuses on tactics to operationalize the strategies outlined in the SEM plan.

Examples of SEM tactical action plans include:
- Fiscal items (student financial aid, scholarships, net tuition revenue)
- Internal communications and data-sharing plan
- Marketing and communications plans
- Recruitment targeted to meet institutional/college/departmental goals including the number of new students (net tuition revenue and capacity), diversity (broadly defined), and profile (academic preparation)
- Student success (retention, engagement, graduation)
- Transfer credit practices/articulation agreements
- Process improvements and technology systems enhancements
- Adjusting academic program mix and delivery modes
- Staff development and training
- Student services (including student customer service philosophy)
- Student development
- Advising services
- Career planning
- Alumni development and services (students who are very satisfied with their experience and are champions of the institution)

Tactical action plans should be developed for all student cohorts, for example, freshman, transfer, graduate/professional.

Answers questions such as How? Who? When? and With what?

Draws on best practices.

Should be updated yearly and refined as needed throughout the current recruitment cycle stages.

A SEM plan differs from a tactical plan in that it establishes *strategies* that outline what an organization needs to do to be successful in achieving its goals. A tactical plan defines the methods used to operationalize the strategies (Sigler 2007).

It is a mistake not to give adequate attention to strategy development. If the enrollment manager does not identify the right strategies, the right tactics will not emerge. Tactics are relatively easy to select if the strategies are correct. The challenge with tactics is their effective execution (Sigler 2007).

While successful SEM leaders recognize the crucial role that an effective SEM plan plays in enrollment success, they are also pragmatic. Seasoned SEM practitioners realize that it is imperative to not be frozen into inaction by the somewhat daunting nature of the plan development. It is important not to let the process of developing a "perfect plan" crowd out delivering expected interim results. It is perfectly acceptable (and probably more the norm than the exception) to focus on building the documents and plans needed for operational success and also build the SEM plan on an ongoing, planning-by-doing basis. Typically, institutions have components of the SEM plan already available in various documents they have developed for operating purposes. The SEM plan can be constructed by placing the various documents, plus the additional information required for the plan, into a comprehensive and coherent narrative.

SEM Tactical Action Plans

Tactical action plans have been a key enrollment-related planning tool for decades. Figure 7 provides an outline of the purpose and components of a SEM tactical plan. The multiple tactical action plans listed reflect the holistic and comprehensive approach of a best-practice SEM program.

While successful SEM leaders recognize the crucial role that effective strategies play in enrollment success, they are also pragmatic. Seasoned SEM practitioners realize that it is imperative to not be frozen into inaction by the somewhat daunting nature of the plan development. It is important not to let the process of developing a "perfect plan" crowd out delivering expected interim results.

Chapter Six:

Transforming an Institution into a SEM Organization[7]

Bob Bontrager and Tom Green observed that "to effectively manage the complexities of SEM requires that planning be organized into manageable components" (2014, 274). In order to achieve this manageability, they developed three frameworks around which to align an institution's SEM processes. These are process, organization, and planning. "Taken together, these frameworks constitute a planning model and roadmap for transforming an institution into a SEM organization" (Bontrager and Green 2012, 274).

SEM Process Framework

Bontrager and Green note that the SEM Process Framework (*see* Figure 8) "emanates from continuous improvement concepts. The feedback loop of gathering data, including and sharing governance, monitoring of results, and adjusting course is one that will be familiar to

---

[7] The material in this chapter draws heavily from Bontrager and Green (2012) and Bontrager and Green (2013).

Figure 8. SEM Process Framework

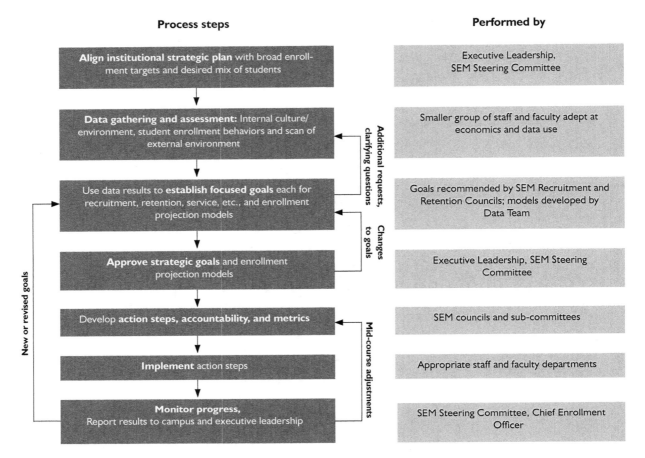

Source: Bontrager and Green (2012).

those who have worked with similar processes in the past, such as accreditation self-studies and strategic plan development" (2012, 274).

The SEM Process Framework outline recommends process steps and who is responsible for completing them. The following are selected extracts of several key points from Bontrager and Green's assessment of this framework.

1. "First, the framework places the setting of enrollment goals within the broader planning framework of the institution" (2012, 275).

2. "The linkage between the institution's strategic plan and the SEM plan must rest at the Executive Leadership level, where the broad vision of the institution is formed and/or translated into operational plans" (2012, 275).

3. "The addition of the SEM steering committee broadens the discussion beyond the executive team and adds the enrollment focus to it" (2012, 275).

4. "Second, the broad enrollment goals and mix of students are researched and supported by data and information that informs the broad goals against internal and external constraints and opportunities. This assures the institution that its decisions are based on sound and thorough research, avoiding planning by anecdote or decisions that are insulated from demographic and market trends" (2012, 275).

5. "Third, the process framework assumes broad involvement of persons across campus, from different administrative levels, departments, and roles, including faculty" (2012, 276).

6. "Establishing *clear expectations for participation* is crucial to a smooth planning process. Councils must know that their role is to develop detailed recommendations and that the decisions to accept them rest with executive leadership, where connection to the broader institutional issues of budget, vision, and governance exists" (2012, 275).

Taken together, these frameworks constitute a planning model and roadmap for transforming an institution into a SEM organization

The broad enrollment goals and mix of students are researched and supported by data and information that informs the broad goals against internal and external constraints and opportunities. This assures the institution that its decisions are based on sound and thorough research, avoiding planning by anecdote or decisions that are insulated from demographic and market trends.

SEM Organizational Framework

College and university faculty, staff, and students value and expect to be consulted about important issues. The wise adage that people support what they help create reflects one of the key expected outcomes of the SEM organizational framework (*see* Figure 9). The organizational model built by Bontrager and Green (2012) represents a vehicle for obtaining broad, cross-functional input and buy-in.

The following are selected extracts of several key points from Bontrager and Green (2012) about this framework:

1. "First, effective SEM planning requires senior-level leadership, reflecting the cross-functional nature of enrollment initiatives and the importance of enrollment outcomes to fulfilling broader institutional goals.

Figure 9. SEM Organizational Framework

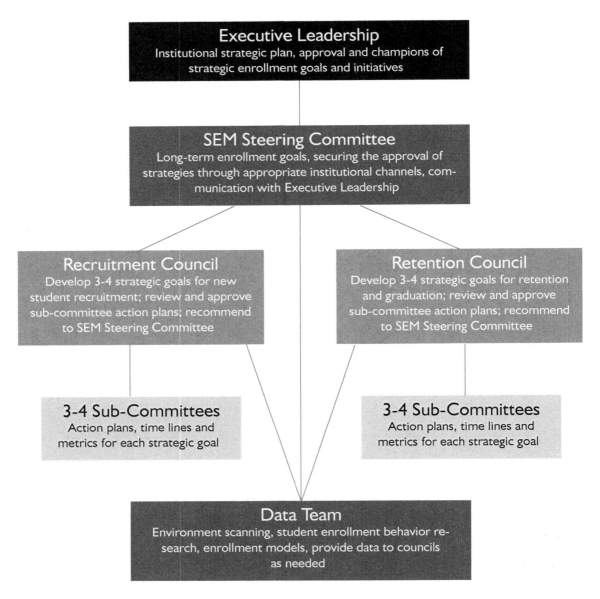

Executive Leadership
Institutional strategic plan, approval and champions of strategic enrollment goals and initiatives

SEM Steering Committee
Long-term enrollment goals, securing the approval of strategies through appropriate institutional channels, communication with Executive Leadership

Recruitment Council
Develop 3-4 strategic goals for new student recruitment; review and approve sub-committee action plans; recommend to SEM Steering Committee

Retention Council
Develop 3-4 strategic goals for retention and graduation; review and approve sub-committee action plans; recommend to SEM Steering Committee

3-4 Sub-Committees
Action plans, time lines and metrics for each strategic goal

3-4 Sub-Committees
Action plans, time lines and metrics for each strategic goal

Data Team
Environment scanning, student enrollment behavior research, enrollment models, provide data to councils as needed

Source: Bontrager and Green (2012).

Placing senior officers from academic affairs, student affairs, and enrollment management as co-chairs of the SEM Steering Committee can establish an important precedent and model for achieving campus-wide engagement,

and the value of doing so" (2012, 277).

2. "Second, recruitment and retention efforts deserve equal attention" (2012, 278).

3. "Finally, the details contained in this organizational framework—partic-

Figure 10. SEM Planning Framework

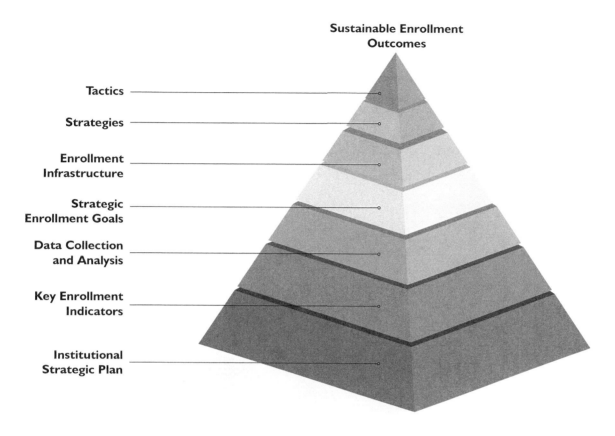

Sustainable Enrollment Outcomes

- Tactics
- Strategies
- Enrollment Infrastructure
- Strategic Enrollment Goals
- Data Collection and Analysis
- Key Enrollment Indicators
- Institutional Strategic Plan

Source: Bontrager and Green (2012).

ularly regarding the composition of the steering committee, councils, sub-committees and data teams—are subject to adjustment depending on the specific needs and context of a given campus" (2012, 278).

SEM Planning Framework

The third model in the Bontrager and Green (2012) SEM approach is the SEM Planning Framework displayed in Figure 10. This framework "… augments the process and organizational frameworks by identifying the primary topical areas to be addressed in SEM planning. By beginning at the bottom of the pyramid and working up, institutions are provided a [road map] for developing SEM plans that will achieve [long-term] results" (2012, 279). As indicated in Figure 10, the end goals of the SEM planning framework are sustainable enrollment outcomes.

Table 3 summarizes Bontrager and Green's (2012 and 2013) recommendations of the topical areas to be addressed in the SEM planning framework and the expected outcomes.

37

Table 3. SEM Planning Framework: Topical Areas and Expected Outcomes

Topical Area to Be Addressed in SEM Planning	Expected Outcomes
Institutional strategic plan	1. Clarity of institutional mission, vision, goals 2. Core competencies 3. Strategic direction 4. Aggregate enrollment goals
Key enrollment indicators (KEIs)	1. Student categories: first year, transfer, dual enrollment, vocational/technical, continuing education, face-to-face, online, certificate, etc. 2. Desired student groups: racial/ethnic diversity, academic ability, first generation 3. Geographic origin: local, regional 4. Recruitment, retention, completion 5. Institutional capacity
Data collection and analysis	1. Internal benchmarks: KEI numbers over the past three to five years 2. Environmental scan: demographics, economics, market opportunities, competition 3. Institutional research plan: designated reports and production schedule
Strategic enrollment goals	1. 5- to 10-year KEI targets 2. Focus: the institution's desired future 3. Based on: mission, data, and environmental scanning
Enrollment infrastructure	1. Staffing: skill sets, strategic development 2. Systems: policies, procedures, technology 3. Capacity for making effective enrollment decisions: positions, reporting lines, committees
Strategies	1. Increase new students of specified types 2. Increase retention rates, specifically by student types 3. Utilize emerging technologies 4. Financial aid/scholarships 5. Academic programs: mix and delivery systems
Tactics	1. Marketing/branding initiatives 2. Academic program review 3. Multilingual recruitment materials 4. Targeted interventions for students in high-risk courses 5. Enhanced academic advising 6. Streamlined admission procedures 7. Purchasing a new client relationship management system

Source: Bontrager and Green (2012 and 2013).

Chapter Seven:

It's About People and Service

Ultimately, effective SEM is not just about metrics and processes, but about people and service. The "main show" of a college or university is its faculty and students. The students are the primary reason an institution exists and the faculty represent the academic core of the institution—teaching, research, and service.

The mission of the staff of a college or university – including the enrollment management unit – is to support the work of its students and faculty. This mission requires the staff to be as good at what they do as the institution's best faculty are at what they do.

Traits of a Successful SEM Leader

SEM is a complex, fast-paced, and high-stakes endeavor. As Richard Ekman, President of the Council of Independent Colleges, recently observed, "If you make a disastrous decision about enrollment strategy, that doesn't go away in six months" (Gardner 2016).

The role of a SEM leader is crucial to an institution's success and is very demanding. As noted in the *Enrollment Management Review*:

> *Successful senior enrollment managers have to operate simultaneously on multiple levels. They need to be up to date, even on the cutting edge of technology, marketing, recruitment, the latest campus practices to enhance student persistence, and financial aid practices. They need to be able to guide and use research to inform institutional practices and strategies. Successful enrollment managers need to be good leaders, managers, and strategic thinkers. They have to have a thorough understanding of the institutions where they work and a realistic assessment of the competitive position in which it resides and the niche within which it can realistically aspire to compete. Furthermore, to be effective, enrollment managers must also have a sense of how public, societal, and competitive forces are likely to move enrollment-related policies and practices in the future.* (2007)

A successful SEM leader holds the following traits:

- A clear understanding of what the SEM program's stakeholders value and expect from the organization and focus on consistently meeting those expectations

- The ability to enlist and maintain the confidence, support, and involvement of key stakeholders in the EM effort
- A strong commitment to working effectively and respectfully with an increasingly diverse student body, work force, and community
- The ability to identify and develop current and emerging talent
- Respect for the unique culture of higher education
- Outstanding communication and political skills
- Strong integrity, ethics, values, and empathy
- The ability to plan at both the strategic and tactical levels
- Emotional intelligence
- The ability to be an effective change agent and to lead the EM unit to continually evolve to effectively carry out its mission
- The ability to develop and lead a SEM program that provides the institution with the optimum chance to consistently meet its enrollment objectives

Survey Results: Responsibilities and Reporting Line of Chief Enrollment Management Officers

In 2014, AACRAO Director of Research Wendy Kilgore conducted a survey of chief enrollment management officers (CEMO).[8]

[8] Details regarding the AACRAO Survey (Chief Enrollment Management Officer Career Profile Report): "The survey was sent electronically to a list of 615 AACRAO members who were selected by their position title as most likely to be the Chief Enrollment Management Officer (CEMO) of their institution. The overall response rate was 24.9% (n = 153). The respondents represented U.S. institutions of varying sizes, control and types."

Table 4. Chief Enrollment Management Officer Portfolio of Responsibilities

	Responsible	Supervise	Participate	Inform	N/A
Recruitment	34.2%	61.2%	2.0%	2.0%	0.7%
Admissions Processing	32.9%	62.5%	3.9%	0.7%	0.0%
Records and registration	18.4%	41.4%	12.5%	19.7%	7.9%
Financial aid	26.3%	55.9%	8.6%	5.3%	3.9%
Retention/student success	21.1%	25.0%	44.7%	5.9%	3.3%
Institutional research	3.3%	8.6%	67.8%	16.4%	3.9%
Enrollment research	50.7%	30.9%	17.8%	0.7%	0.0%
Academic advising	5.3%	14.5%	25.7%	38.8%	15.8%
Academic skills support	2.0%	8.6%	19.7%	34.9%	34.9%
Career services	4.6%	13.8%	13.8%	32.2%	35.5%
Recruitment marketing	32.9%	48.7%	13.2%	2.0%	3.3%
Institutional marketing	12.5%	15.8%	62.5%	5.9%	3.3%
Institutional enrollment goals	73.0%	12.5%	11.2%	1.3%	2.0%
Academic college/department enrollment goals	25.7%	13.2%	40.8%	16.4%	3.9%
Veteran services	12.5%	30.3%	28.9%	13.2%	15.1%

Source: AACRAO Survey of Chief Enrollment Management Officers Profile Report (Kilgore 2014).

Figure 11. Chief Enrollment Management Officer (CEMO) Reporting Line

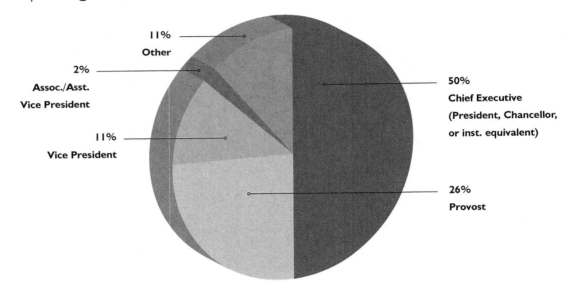

11%
Other

2%
Assoc./Asst.
Vice President

11%
Vice President

50%
Chief Executive
(President, Chancellor,
or inst. equivalent)

26%
Provost

Source: AACRAO Survey of Chief Enrollment Management Officers Profile Report (Kilgore 2014).

Table 4 provides insight into the duties of the CEMO. Figure 11 indicates the reporting lines for the CEMO. The survey results indicate that:

In the aggregate, half (50.3%) of respondents report directly to the chief executive officer (CEO) of the institution and one quarter (25.5%) report to the provost... Among private, non-profit institutions 76% report directly to the CEO whereas only 30% of respondents from public institutions reported to that level. The

most common reporting line at public institutions is to the provost (38%). In this sample, we found that it is more likely for the chief enrollment management position to report to the CEO at smaller institutions. Only 8% of respondents from institutions with an enrollment of 20,000+ report to the CEO. On the other end of the scale, 83% of respondents from institutions with fewer than 1,000 students report to the CEO. (Kilgore 2014)[9]

[9] This section of the survey was designed to capture chief enrollment management officer functional responsibilities and to attempt to gauge levels of involvement in each function. Dr. Kilgore created a list of 14 functions from which respondents chose and she defined levels of involvement as follows:
a. Responsible = not a delegated function
b. Supervise = delegated and supervised
c. Participate = neither supervise nor delegate but influence decisions related to that function
d. Inform = relay information about a function but have no decision-making influence or authority

The demand for highly proficient SEM leaders is very high. In contrast, the current pool of those who can lead a consistently high-performing SEM program is fairly small. Top SEM leaders can command salaries and benefits that are among the highest for the administrative leadership at the institution. They can expect to have direct access to the highest levels of leadership at an institution and to give input on major institutional decisions.

College and university trustees and senior leaders would be well advised to intentionally identify persons at their institution who hold the potential to develop into successful senior enrollment managers. Institutional leaders should then help these individuals develop the necessary skills and successful experience to move into a senior enrollment manager role at the institution. Some resources that will aid in the professional development of these highly important institutional leaders are listed on page 47.

High-achieving SEM leaders fully understand that successful SEM is about building relationships and teamwork. The role of a symphony orchestra conductor provides an excellent metaphor for the role of the SEM leader. Just as the conductor focuses the

> The role of a symphony orchestra conductor provides an excellent metaphor for the role of the SEM leader. Leading a SEM program is not about control but coordination.

orchestra on her/his vision of how the music should sound and conducts the performance accordingly, so, too, the SEM leader involves the organizational components of the entire institution in the SEM program. Leading a SEM program is not about control but coordination. The SEM leader – with the direct involvement and support of the institution's senior leadership – orchestrates, via the SEM plan, the timing of when each component of the institution contributes its unique skills and talents toward achieving the institution's enrollment-related goals and student success.

Conclusion:

Taking Control of Your Enrollment Destiny

"People can be divided into three groups:
Those who make things happens,
Those who watch things happen,
Those who wonder, 'What happened?'"
(Butler/Newberry 1987)

Enrollment is the lifeblood of almost all colleges and universities. It has a direct impact on the ability of an institution to carry out its mission. The enrollment picture of a college or university also directly influences its vitality and the perception of the institution. Making the choice whether to make things happen, watch things happen, or wonder 'what happened?' can have a major impact on an institution's enrollment destiny.

Peter Drucker, widely credited as the "father" of modern business management,

maintained that the most important task of an organization's leader is to perhaps not avert crisis, but to anticipate it (Drucker 1990). Waiting until the crisis hits to address it is equated to abdicating. A true leader has to make the organization capable of anticipating the storm, weathering it, and, in fact, being ahead of it. This, Drucker says, calls for innovation and constant renewal.

In addition to Drucker's description of a leader's critical duties, an effective leader must also offer direction and hope. As a long-time enrollment practitioner and consultant, I find that the world of competitive sports offers a very visible and fitting analogy to the choice colleges and universities face in addressing the challenges of the "new normal." While sports enthusiasts can debate for hours as to whether a good offense or a good defense wins championships, in reality, it's probably having both an effective offense and defense that help teams consistently enjoy success (Sigler 2007). A team that has to unduly play defense is often described as being "back on its heels" because it is largely retreating instead of controlling its own destiny. This leads to inordinate fatigue and discouragement. Teams that are playing offense play off the balls of their feet because they are intent on moving forward to make good things happen. Playing offense is much more joyful because it focuses on making good things happen and helping the organization better shape its destiny.

SEM is neither a quick fix nor a silver bullet. It is challenging to install and operate, but when implemented effectively, it can be a powerful proactive tool to help an institution take better control of its enrollment destiny. In the words of Harvard Business professor Michael Porter, while luck and intuition are both alive and well, "human beings have some control over their own destiny. And you can improve your odds of making better judgments [through good strategy]" (Surowiecki, 1999). Indeed, strategic enrollment management can improve a college or university's odds of making better judgments.

Appendix A: Strategic Enrollment Management Resources

Publications

www.aacrao.org/bookstore

Handbook of Strategic Enrollment Management (2014)

Leadership Lessons: Vision and Values for a New Generation (2013)

Strategic Enrollment Management: Transforming Higher Education (2012)

SEM in Canada: Promoting Student and Institutional Success in Canadian Colleges and Universities (2011)

Applying SEM at the Community College (2009)

SEM and Institutional Success: Integrating Enrollment, Finance and Student Access (2008)

Conferences

www.aacrao.org/professional-development/meetings/current-meetings

AACRAO Strategic Enrollment Management Conference

Certifications

www.aacrao.org/professional-development/strategic-enrollment-management-endorsement-program

Strategic Enrollment Management Endorsement Program

Journals

www.aacrao.org/resources/publications/sem-quarterly

SEM Quarterly

47

Appendix B: Internal Enrollment Management Assessment Template[10]

Using your knowledge of your institution, provide your opinion as to how your institution performs on each of the strategic enrollment management (SEM) components. The template uses a 5-point assessment scale, with 5 being excellent and with 1 being poor. Place an "X" in the appropriate column for each component. You may also evaluate the subtopics under each component

[10] adapted by Clayton Smith, Associate Professor, University of Windsor.

49

SEM Components	Poor to Excellent				
	1	2	3	4	5

1. Align institutional strategic plan with broad enrollment targets and desired mix of students, including:
 	
  • Clarity of institutional mission, vision, goals
 	
  • Clarity of unit/program within institutional mission
 	
  • Strategic direction
 	
  • Aggregate enrollment goals
 	
Comments:					

2. Achieve an institutional culture of partnership and collaboration, including leadership, participation, and buy-in from:
 	
  • Overall campus community
 	
  • Top-level administrators
 	
  • Academic colleges/faculties and departments
 	
  • Student service units
 	
  • Academic support programs and centers for underserved populations
 	
  • Information technology
 	
  • Student unions and organizations
 	
Comments:					

SEM Components	Poor to Excellent				
	1	2	3	4	5

3. Establish clear 5- to 10-year key enrollment indicator (KEI) targets for the number and types of students needed to fulfill the institutional mission:
 	
  • Student categories: first year, transfer, graduate, dual enrollment, vocational/technical, continuing education, etc.
 	
  • Desired student groups: racial/ethnic diversity, academic ability/quality, first generation
 	
  • Geographic origin: local, regional
 	
  • Student engagement scores
 	
  • Student retention rate
 	
  • Graduation rate
 	
  • Institutional and program capacity
 	
  • Learning modality (online, blended learning, experiential education)
 	
Comments:					

SEM Components	Poor to Excellent				
	1	2	3	4	5

4. Create a data-rich environment to inform decisions and evaluate strategies. Data collection and analysis includes:
 	
• Willingness to review institutional and student data
 	
• KEI numbers over the past three to five years
 	
• Environmental scan:
  - Demographics
  - Economics
  - Market opportunities
  - Competition
 	
• Tracking of admissions (recruitment and registration yields)
 	
• Tracking of student persistence and graduation rates
 	
• Use of student satisfaction or engagement surveys
 	
• Providing designated reports using consistent formats and definitions on an established production schedule to campus and executive leadership
 	
• Use of data results to establish focused goals for recruitment, retention, service, etc., and enrollment projection models
 	
Comments:					

SEM Components	Poor to Excellent				
	1	2	3	4	5
5. Develop an enrollment infrastructure sufficient to achieve enrollment targets, including: • Staffing: skill sets, strategic development • Systems: policies, procedures, technology • Capacity for making effective enrollment decisions: positions, reporting lines, committees • Accountability and metrics for achieving SEM goals Comments:					
6. Enable effective financial planning and generate added net revenue for the institution: • Budget planning is coordinated and strategically allocated to support short-term and long-range enrollment goals. Comments:					

SEM Components	Poor to Excellent				
	1	2	3	4	5
7. Develop strategies for achieving KEI targets and enhancing student success by assisting students to effectively and efficiently transition from prospective student status through the student enrollment life cycle to enrollment, retention, and graduation: • Increase new students of specified types • Increase retention rates, specifically by student types • Utilize emerging technologies • Use financial aid strategically to support enrollment goals • Deliver effective academic programs (mix and delivery systems) • Promote academic success by improving student access, transition, persistence, and graduation • Increase process and organizational efficiency • Improve service levels to all stakeholders (e.g., prospective and current students, other institutional departments, other institutions, coordinating agencies) Comments:					

SEM Components	Poor to Excellent				
	1	2	3	4	5
8. Implement action steps/tactics for implementing enrollment-related strategies, including: • Marketing/branding initiatives - Institutional differentiation and "branding" - Coordination of marketing materials - Integration of marketing and communications plan • Academic program review • Creating multilingual recruitment materials • Targeted interventions for students in high-risk courses • Enhanced academic advising • Streamlined admission and registration procedures • Implementing/supporting a client relationship management system • Using electronic/virtual student services and technology to support related internal business processes • Strengthening international student processes and services Comments:					

SEM Components	Poor to Excellent				
	1	2	3	4	5
9. Achieve sustainable institutional SEM by: • Use of an institutional SEM plan, which includes an ongoing review and assessment process, for determining, achieving, and maintaining optimum enrollment over the long term • Ensuring the organizational structures supporting SEM planning and implementation work well • Creating and continuously strengthening linkages with functions and activities across the campus • Enabling effective campus-wide planning: - Revisions to the institutional strategic plan - Academic planning: curriculum, faculty needs - Facility planning - Financial planning Comments:					

Bibliography

Bontrager, B. 2004. Enrollment management: An introduction to concepts and structures. *College and University*. 79(3):11-6.

Bontrager, B. 2006. *The Brave New World of Strategic Enrollment Management*. Retrieved 2017 from: <consulting.aacrao.org>. Washington, DC: American Association of Collegiate Registrars and Admissions Officers.

Bontrager, B. 2011. Achieving student and institutional goals through strategic enrollment management. *Enhancing Enrollment and Financial Outcomes*, 10 and 11. San Diego, CA: American Association of Collegiate Registrars and Admissions Officers.

Bontrager, B., and T. Green 2012. A structure for SEM planning. In *Strategic Enrollment Management: Transforming Higher Education*, edited by B. Bontrager, D. Ingersoll, and R. Ingersoll.. Washington, DC: American Association of Collegiate Registrars and Admissions Officers, 273-84.

Bontrager, B., and T. Green, " SEM Planning Frameworks." Presentation at the AACRAO Strategic Enrollment Management Conference, Chicago, IL, November 13-10, 2013.

Butler, Nicholas Murray, Address to the University of California, March 23, 1931. Retrieved March 2, 2017 from <http://www.barrypopik.com/index.php/new_york_city/entry/those_who_make_things_happen_those_who_watch_things_happen_and_those_who_wo>

Campanella, F. 1974 (November). Papers of J. Maguire. Boston, MA.

Davenport, T. H., and J. G. Harris. 2007. *Competing on Analytics: The New Science of Winning*. Cambridge, MA: Harvard Business School Press.

Dolence, M. 1993. *Strategic Enrollment Management: A Primer for Campus Administrators*. Washington, DC: American Association of Collegiate Registrars and Admissions Officers.

Dolence, M. 1999. Phone interview with S. E. Henderson. Cincinnati, OH.

Enrollment Management Review, The. 2007 (Fall). *CollegeBoard.com*. Edited by D. Hossler, L. Hoezee, and D. Rogalski. Retrieved Jan. 10, 2017, from: <CollegeBoard.com>. *The Enrollment Management Review*. 23(1).

Gage, B., and W. Sigler, "SEM Core Concepts and SEM Planning for Teams." Presentation at the AACRAO Strategic Enrollment Management Conference, November 6-9, 2016.

Gardner, L. 2016 (November 25). Getting Up to Speed as a New President. *The Chronicle of Higher Education*.

Gottheil, S., and C. Smith. 2011. *SEM in Canada*. Washington, DC: American Association of Collegiate Registrars and Admissions Officers.

Green, T. 2016b (April). *Strategic Enrollment Management Quarterly*, edited by T. Green and H. Zimar. Retrieved from: <http://onlinelibrary.wiley.com/journal/10.1002/(ISSN)2325-4750>.

Green, T. 2016 (August). Discussion via email with author.

Haycock, K. 2006. *Promise Abandoned: How Policy Choices and Institutional Practices Restrict College Opportunities*. Washington, DC: The Education Trust.

Henderson, S. 2001. On the brink of a profession. In *The Strategic Enrollment Management Revolution*, edited by J. Black. Washington, DC: American Association of Collegiate Registrars and Admissions Officers, p. 16.

Henderson, S. 2005. Refocusing enrollment management: Losing structure and finding the academic context. *College and University*. 80(3):3-8.

Henderson, S. 2012. Integrating evolving perspectives: The roots and wings of enrollment management. In *Strategic Enrollment Management: Transforming Higher Education*, edited by B. Bontrager, D. Ingersoll, and R. Ingersoll. Washington, DC: American Association of Collegiate Registrars and Admissions Officers.

Henderson, S. 2012. The community of SEM. In *Strategic Enrollment Management: Transforming Higher Education*, edited by B. Bontrager, D. Ingersoll, and R. Ingersoll. Washington, DC: American Association of Collegiate Registrars and Admissions Officers.

Henderson, S., and A. Yale. "Enrollment Management 101." Presentation at the AACRAO Strategic Enrollment Management Conference, November 16-19, 2008.

Hossler, D. 1986. *Creating Effective Enrollment Management Systems*. New York: The College Board.

Hossler, D. 2011. From admissions to enrollment management. In *Rentz's Student Affairs Practice in Higher Education*, 4th ed., edited by F. M. Associates. Springfield, IL: Charles C. Thomas.

Hossler, D., and J. Bean. 1990. *The Strategic Management of College Enrollments*. San Francisco: Jossey-Bass.

Hossler, D., and D. Kalsbeek. 2008. Enrollment management: Managing enrollments. *College and University*. 83(4):6.

Huddleston, T. 1980. In consideration of marketing and reorganization. *The National Association of College Admissions Counselors Journal*. 25(1).

Kalsbeek, D. 2006. Some reflections on SEM structures and strategies (part one). *College and University*. 81(3):3-10.

Kalsbeek, D. 2006. Some reflections on SEM structures and strategies (part two). *College and University*. 81(4):3-10.

Kalsbeek, D. 2007. Some reflections on SEM structures and strategies (part three). *College and University*. 82(3):3-12.

Kemerer, F. R., J. Baldridge, and K. Green. 1982. *Strategies for Effective Enrollment Management*. Washington, DC: American Association of State Colleges and Universities.

Kerlin, C. 2008. A community college roadmap for the enrollment management journey. *College and University*. 83(4):11.

Kilgore, W. 2014. *Chief Enrollment Management Officer Career Profile Report*. Retrieved Jan. 16, 2017, from: <http://www.aacrao.org/docs/default-source/PDF-Files/aacrao-chief-enrollment-management-office-career-profile-report-june-2014.pdf?sfvrsn=2>. Washington, DC: American Association of Collegiate Registrars and Admissions Officers.

Michaelson, G. A. 1987. *Winning the Marketing War: A Field Manual for Business Leaders*. Lanham, MD: Abt Books.

Norris, D. and L. Baer, n.d. *A Toolkit for Building Organizational Capacity for Analytics*. Herndon, VA: Strategic Initiatives, Inc. Retrieved March 6, 2017 from https://docs.google.com/file/d/0B0C-geHHcp-YzMEZPY2hCRHpyLVU/edit.

Online Business Dictionary. n.d. SWOT analysis. Retrieved 2017 from: <http://www.businessdictionary.com/definition/SWOT-analysis.html>.

Penn, G. 1999. Enrollment Management for the 21st Century: Institutional Goals, Accountability, and Fiscal Responsibility. ASHE-ERIC Higher Education Report. 26(7). (ED430445).

Sigler, W. 2007. *Managing for Outcomes: Shifting from Process-centric to Results-Oriented Operations*. Washington, DC: American Association of Collegiate Registrars and Admissions Officers.

Sigler, W. 2016. *Delivering Outcomes through SEM Processes*, edited by T. Green. Retrieved June 14, 2016, from: <www.aacrao.org/resources/resources-list-view/aacrao-connect>.

Smith, C., and W. Kilgore. 2006. Enrollment Planning: A Workshop on the Development of a SEM Plan. Washington, DC: American Association of Collegiate Registrars and Admissions Officers.

Suters, E. T. 1976. *Succeed in Spite of Yourself*. New York: Van Nostrand Reinhold.